How to paint on Rocks

STEP BY STEP
INSTRUCTIONS

tree

1. CHOOSE A SUITABLE STONE FOR YOUR MOTIF

2. PRIME THE STONE WITH A COLOR OF YOUR CHOICE

3. START WITH THE TREETOP

4. DRAW THE TRUNK

5. DRAW THE LEAVES IN DIFFERENT COLORS

6. A FEW MORE DETAILS MAKE IT LOOK MORE REALISTIC

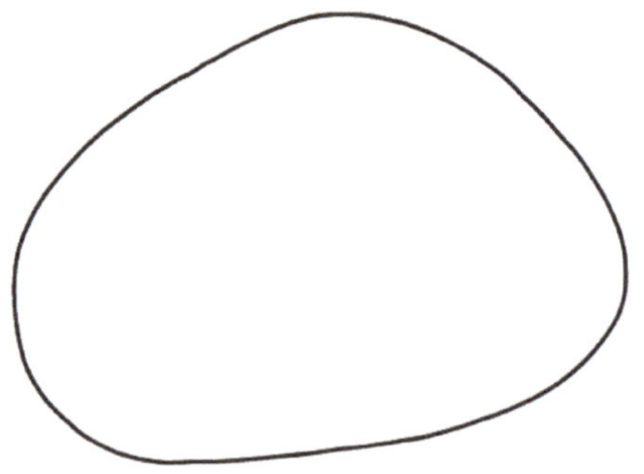

7. TRY IT :)

TIP:

A SPONGE IS IDEAL TO ACHIEVE A WIPING EFFECT LIKE IN POINT 3

bear

1. LOOK FOR THE RIGHT SHAPE FOR YOUR MOTIF

2. PRIME THE STONE

3. DRAW A ROUGH SHAPE OF THE BEAR

4. DRAW THE MOUTH AND EARS

5. DRAW THE EYES AND THE NOSE

6. DETAILS COMPLETE THE PICTURE

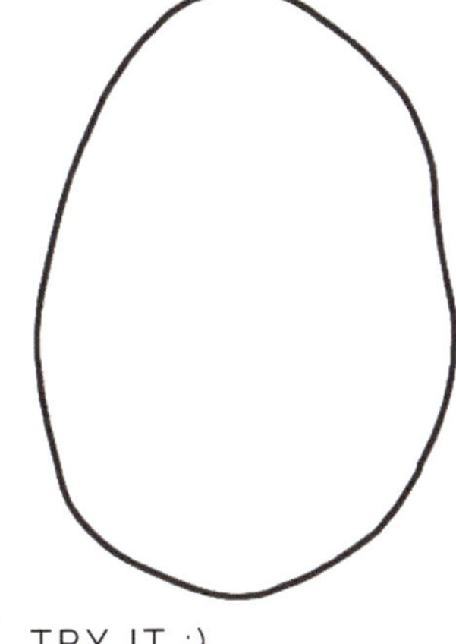

7. TRY IT :)

TIP:

IF YOU PRIME THE STONE BEFOREHAND IN ANY COLOR AS IN POINT 2. THE COLORS COME OUT BETTER AFTERWARDS BUT OF COURSE IT IS NOT A MUST :)

mountains

1. LOOK FOR THE RIGHT SHAPE FOR YOUR MOTIF

2. PRIME THE STONE WITH A COLOR OF YOUR CHOICE

3. DRAWING ROUGH SHAPE OF MOUNTAINS

4. DRAW THE SNOW OF THE MOUNTAINS

5. IT LOOKS MORE REALISTIC WITH CLOUDS AND HIGHLIGHTS

6. TRY IT :)

TIP:

TO MAKE IT EASIER FOR YOU, YOU CAN ROUGHLY DRAW THE MOTIFS WITH A PENCIL

bird

1. LOOK FOR THE RIGHT SHAPE FOR YOUR MOTIF

2. PRIME THE STONE WITH A COLOR OF YOUR CHOICE

3. PAINT ROUGH SHAPE OF BODY

4. DRAW THE FIRST DETAILS

5. GAMES WITH LIGHT AND DARK COLORS THAT GIVE MORE DIMENSION

6. OUTLINE THE INDIVIDUAL ELEMENTS

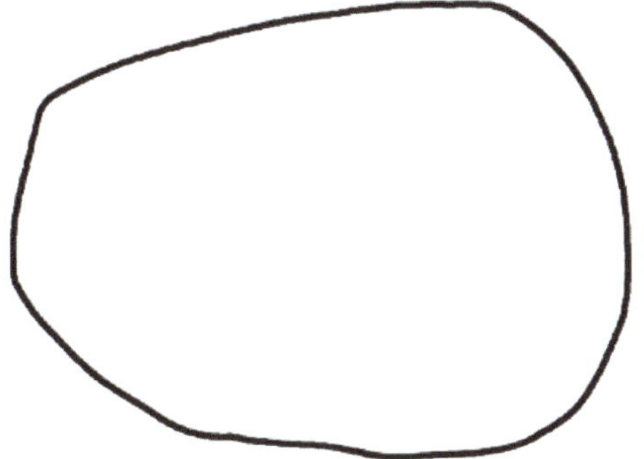

7. TRY IT :)

TIP:

SMALL FILIGREE THINGS ARE BEST DRAWN WITH A FELT PEN OR A THIN BRUSH

Cat face

1. LOOK FOR THE RIGHT STONE FOR YOUR MOTIF

2. PRIME THE STONE WITH A COLOR OF YOUR CHOICE

3. DRAW THE MOUTH AND EYES

4. DRAW THE EYES GREEN

5. DRAW THE WHISKERS AND EYELASHES

6. A FEW MORE FINE HAIRS AND YOU'RE DONE

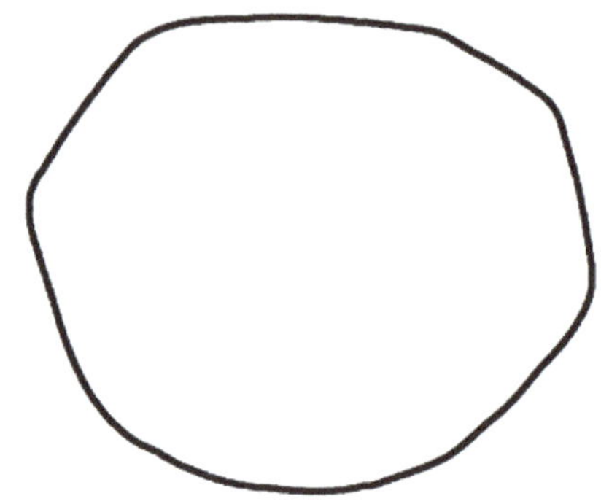

7. TRY IT :)

TIP:

DETAILS LIKE TINY HAIRS MAKE THE MOTIF LOOK MORE REALISTIC

boat

1. LOOK FOR THE RIGHT STONE FOR YOUR MOTIF

2. PRIME THE STONE WITH A COLOR OF YOUR CHOICE

3. DRAW THE WATER

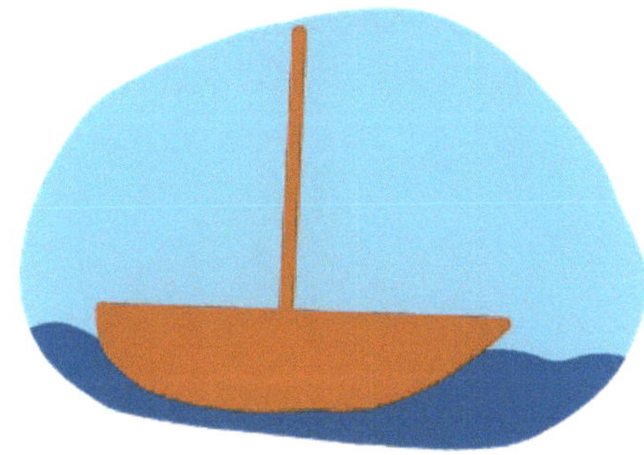

4. DRAW THE BOAT AND THE MAST

5. PAINT THE SAIL AND THE CLOUDS

6. DRAW A FEW LIGHT LINES ON THE BOAT

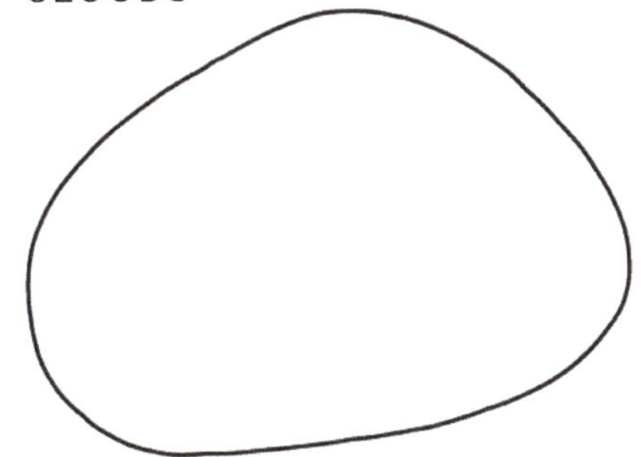

7. TRY IT :)

TIP:

THROUGH UPS AND DOWNS, THE MOTIFS BECOME MORE REALISTIC, E.G. AT POINT 6.

cocktail

1. LOOK FOR THE RIGHT STONE FOR YOUR MOTIF

2. PRIME THE STONE WITH A COLOR OF YOUR CHOICE

3. FIRST PAINT THE CONTENTS OF THE GLASS

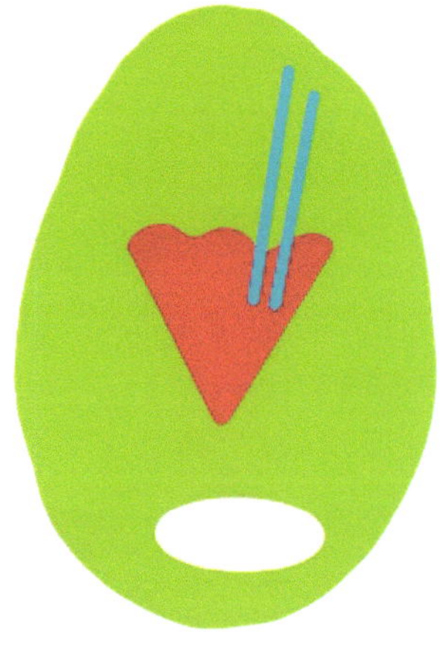

4. THEN DRAW THE FOOT AND THE STRAWS

5. NEXT THE LEMON

6. FINALLY, THE GLASS AND A FEW MORE DETAILS

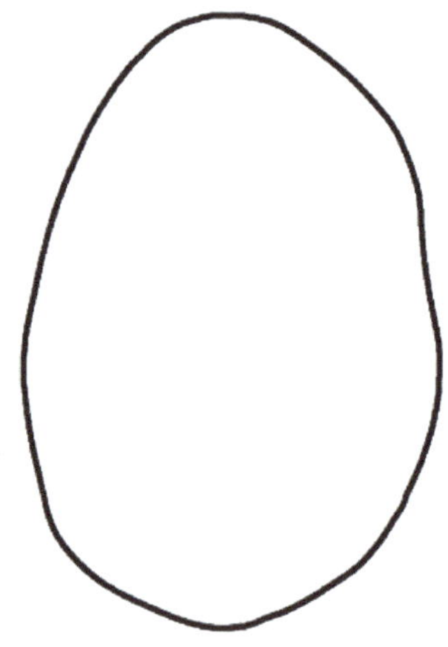

7. TRY IT :)

TIP:

THE FINISHED STONE CAN THEN BE SEALED WITH A CLEAR VARNISH THEN THE COLORS WILL NOT FADE

lighthouse

1. LOOK FOR THE RIGHT STONE FOR YOUR MOTIF

2. PRIME THE STONE

3. FIRST DRAW THE WATER THEN THE TRUNK

4. DRAW THE LIGHTHOUSE

5. FINALLY, THE DETAILS

6. TRY IT :)

TIP:

WHEN CHOOSING THE STONE, ALWAYS PAY ATTENTION TO WHAT KIND OF MOTIF YOU WANT TO PAINT IN THIS CASE A LONG NARROW STONE IS BEST

Hot air balloon

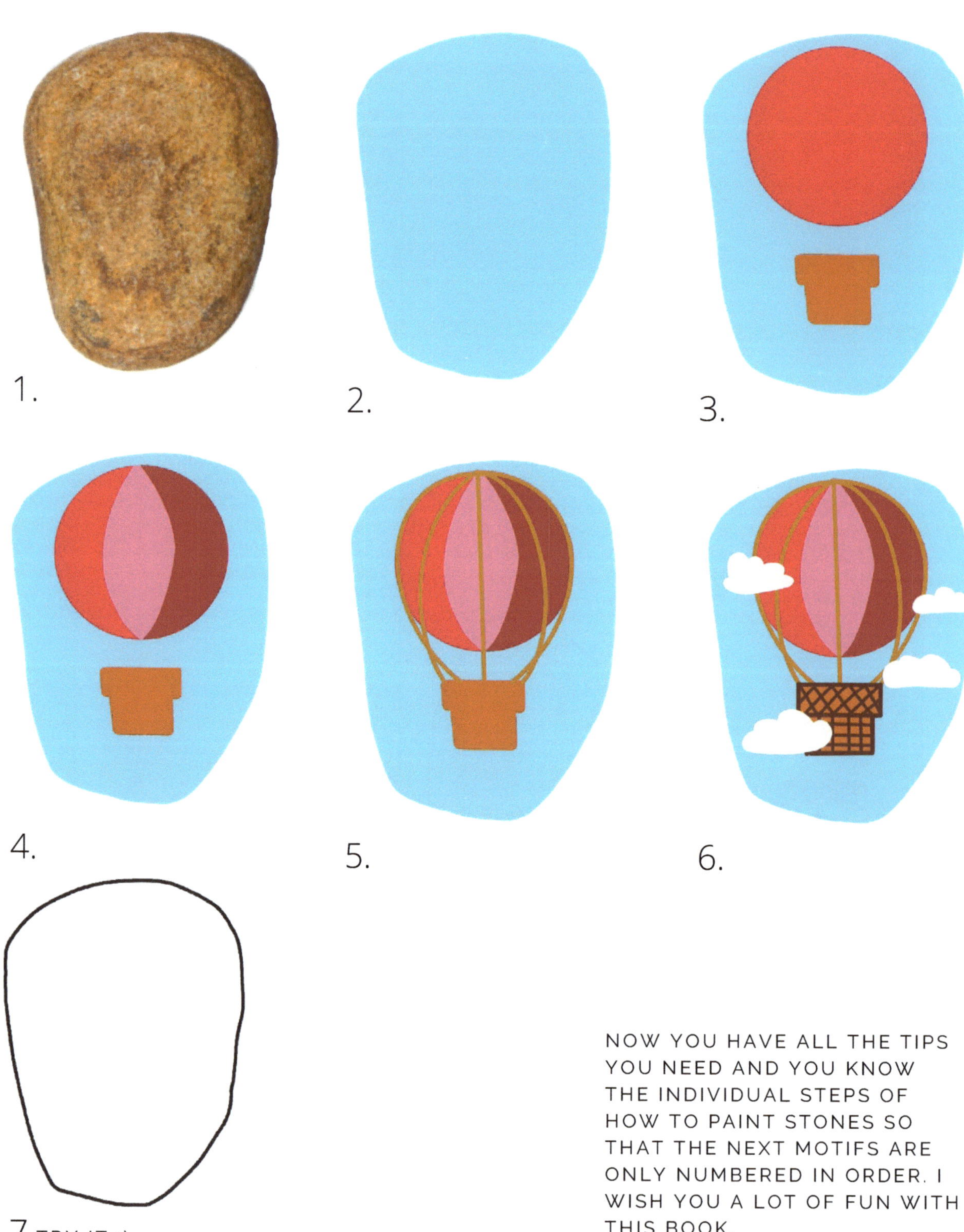

NOW YOU HAVE ALL THE TIPS YOU NEED AND YOU KNOW THE INDIVIDUAL STEPS OF HOW TO PAINT STONES SO THAT THE NEXT MOTIFS ARE ONLY NUMBERED IN ORDER. I WISH YOU A LOT OF FUN WITH THIS BOOK.

cancer

butterfly

cactus

1.

2.

3.

4.

5.

6.

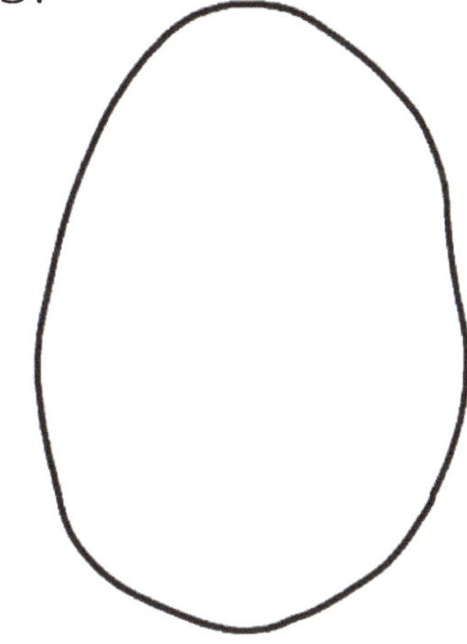

7. TRY IT :)

ice
1.
2.
3.
4.
5.
6.
7. TRY IT :)

owl
1.
2.
3.
4.
5.
6.
7.
8. TRY IT :)

mushroom

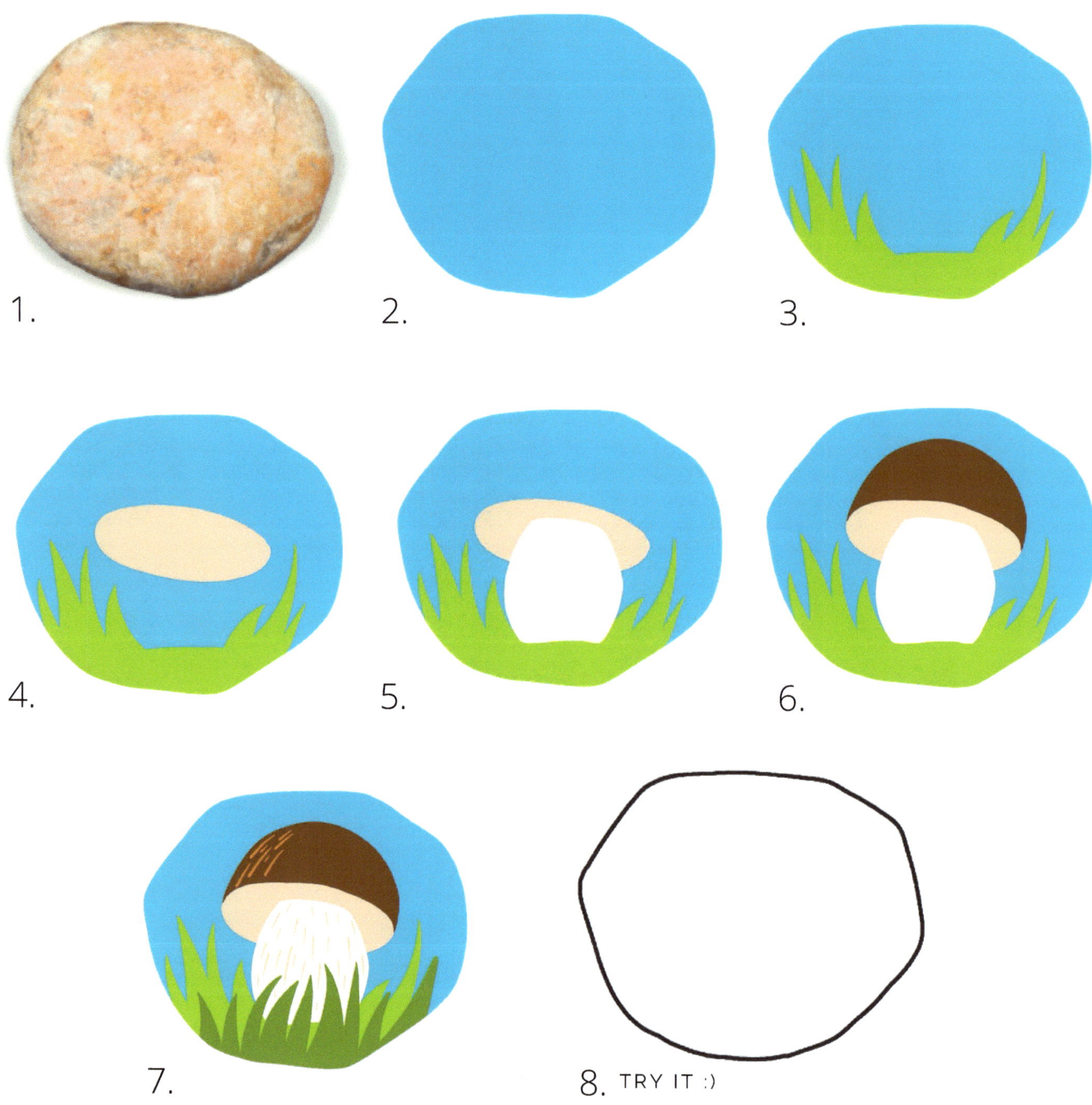

pumpkin

honeycomb

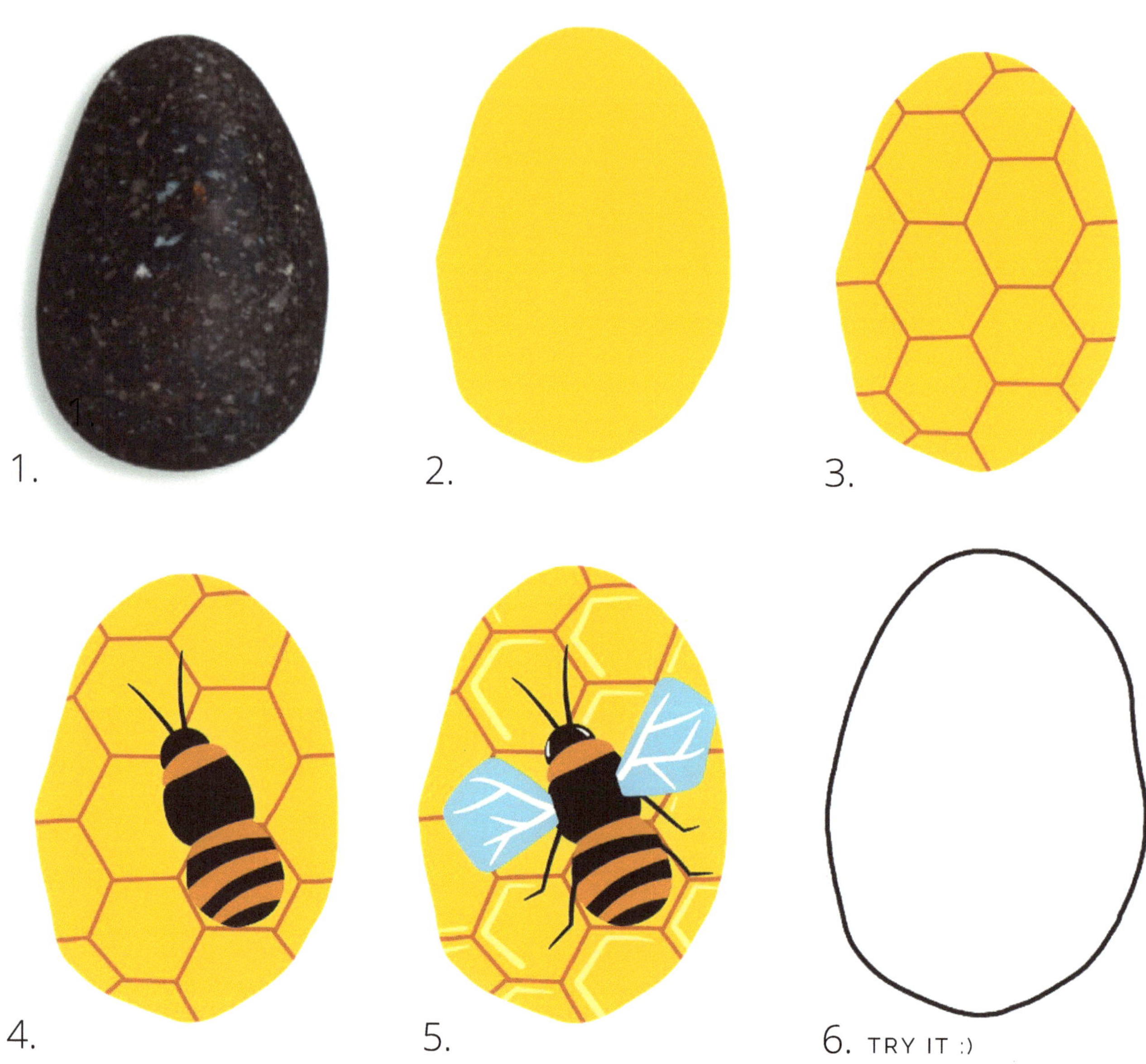

Branch with leaves

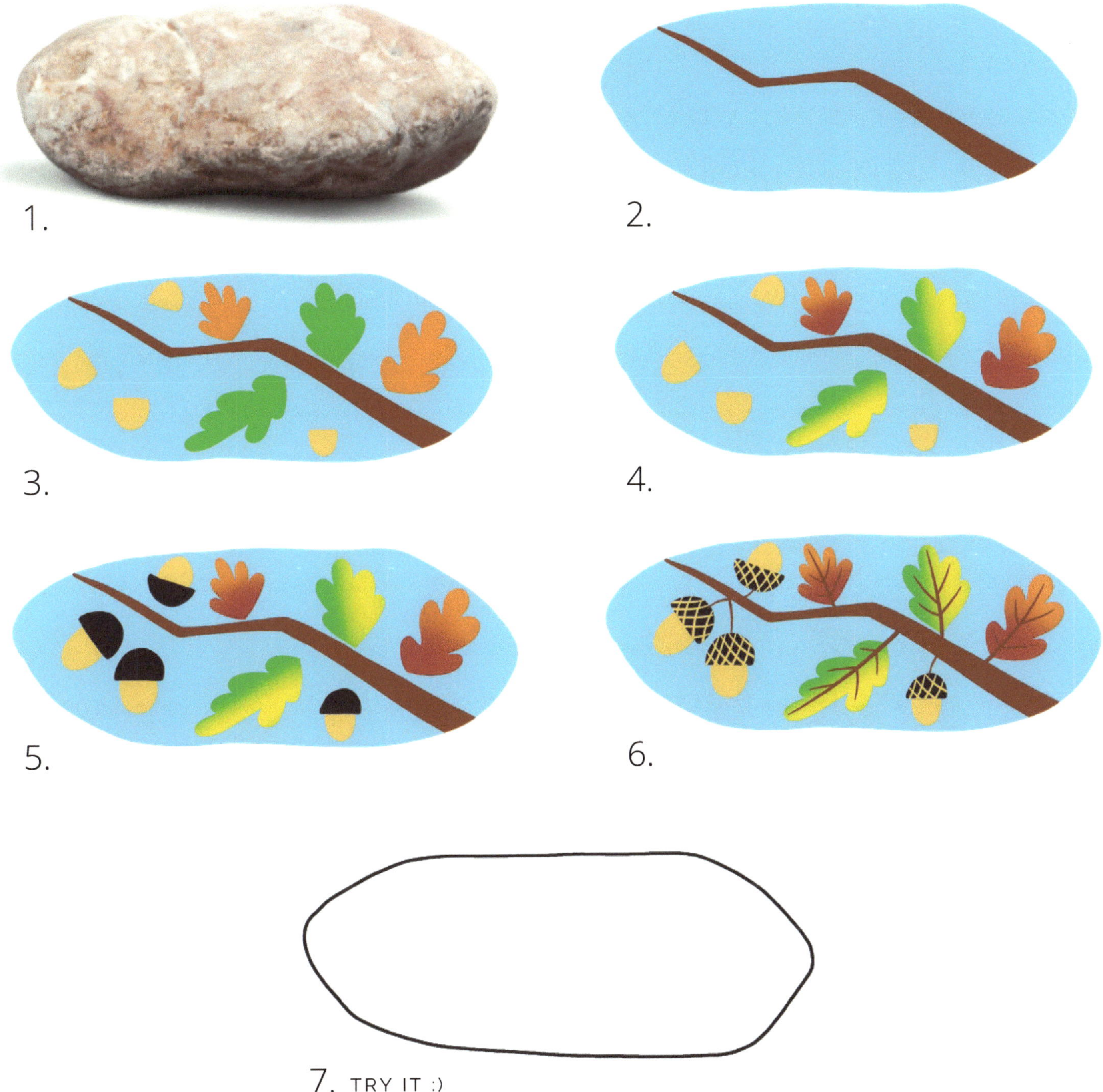

Flowers

Cupcake

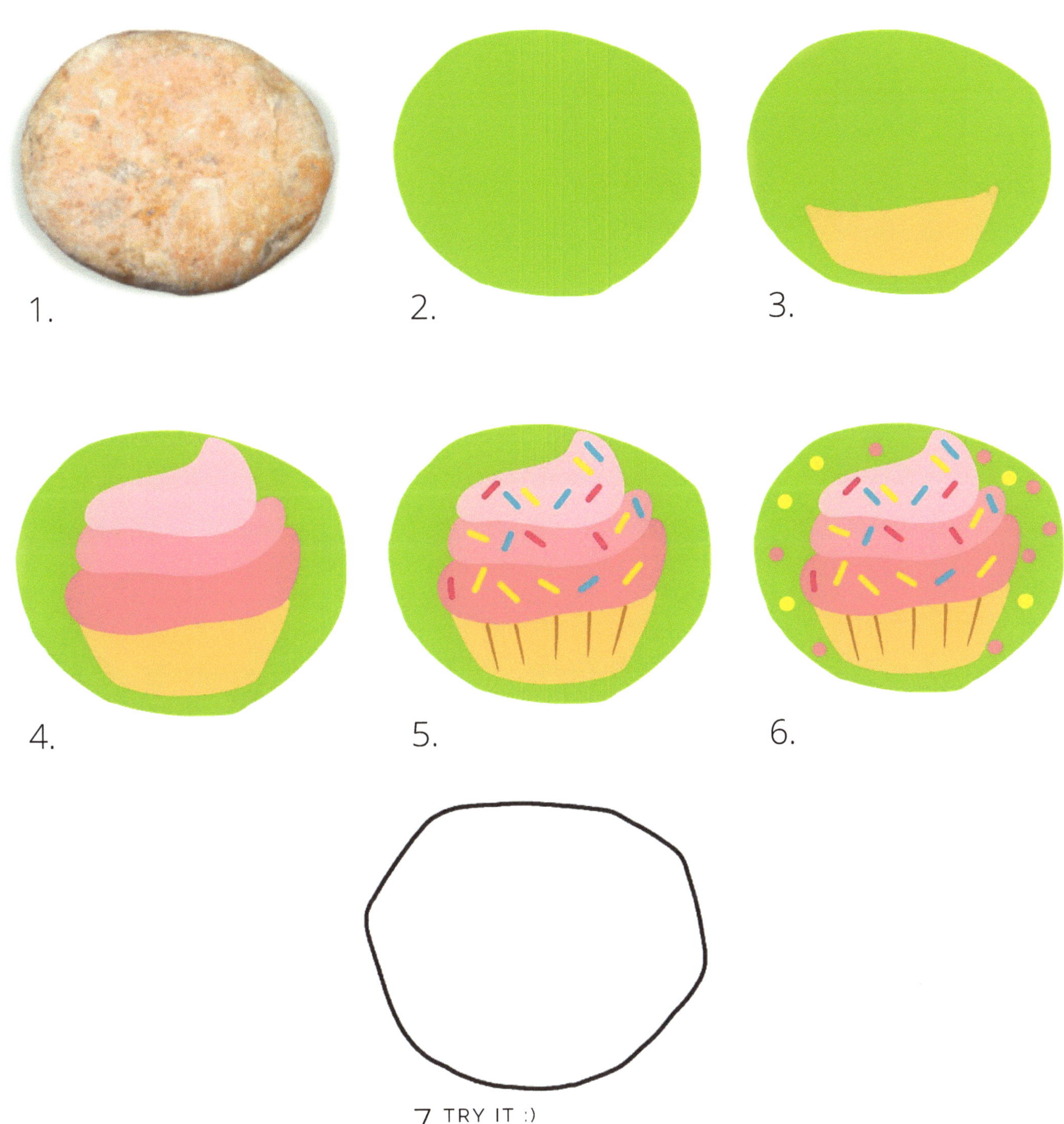

landscape

Water lilies

jellyfish

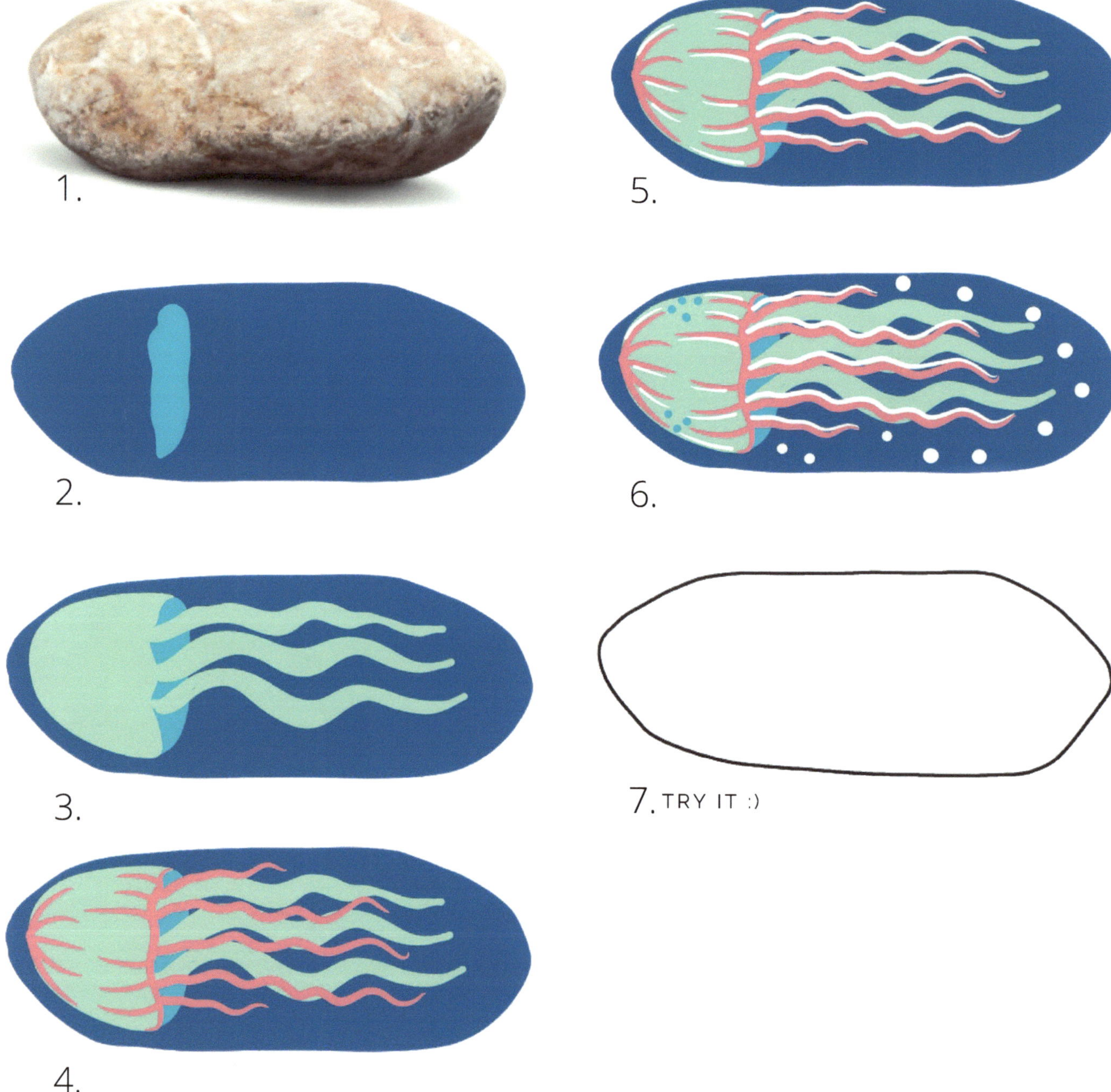

lemon

cat

1.
3.
5.
7.

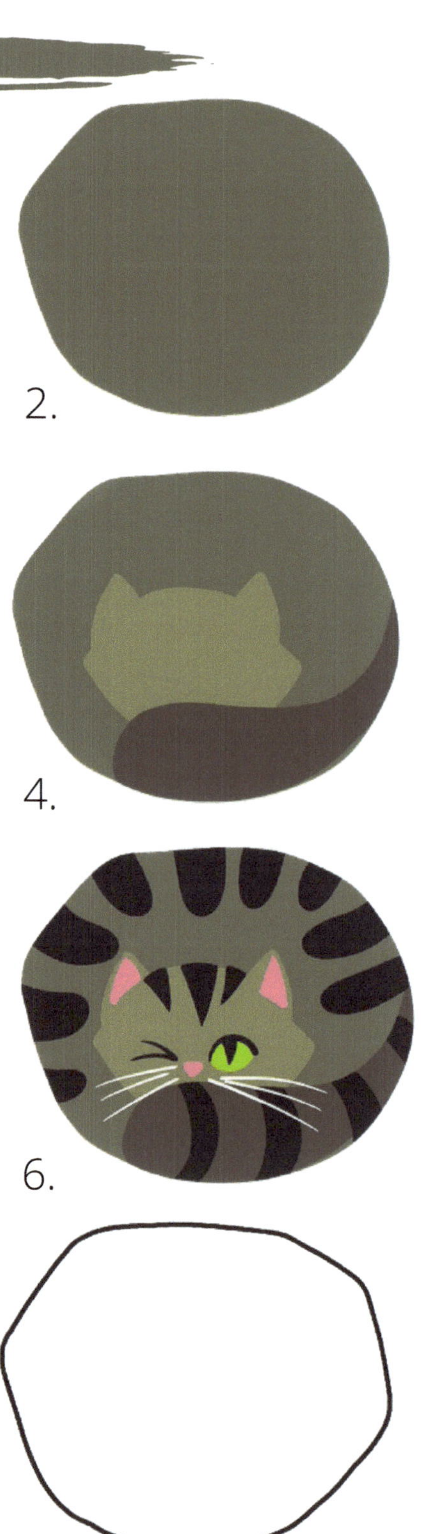
2.
4.
6.
8. TRY IT :)

fish

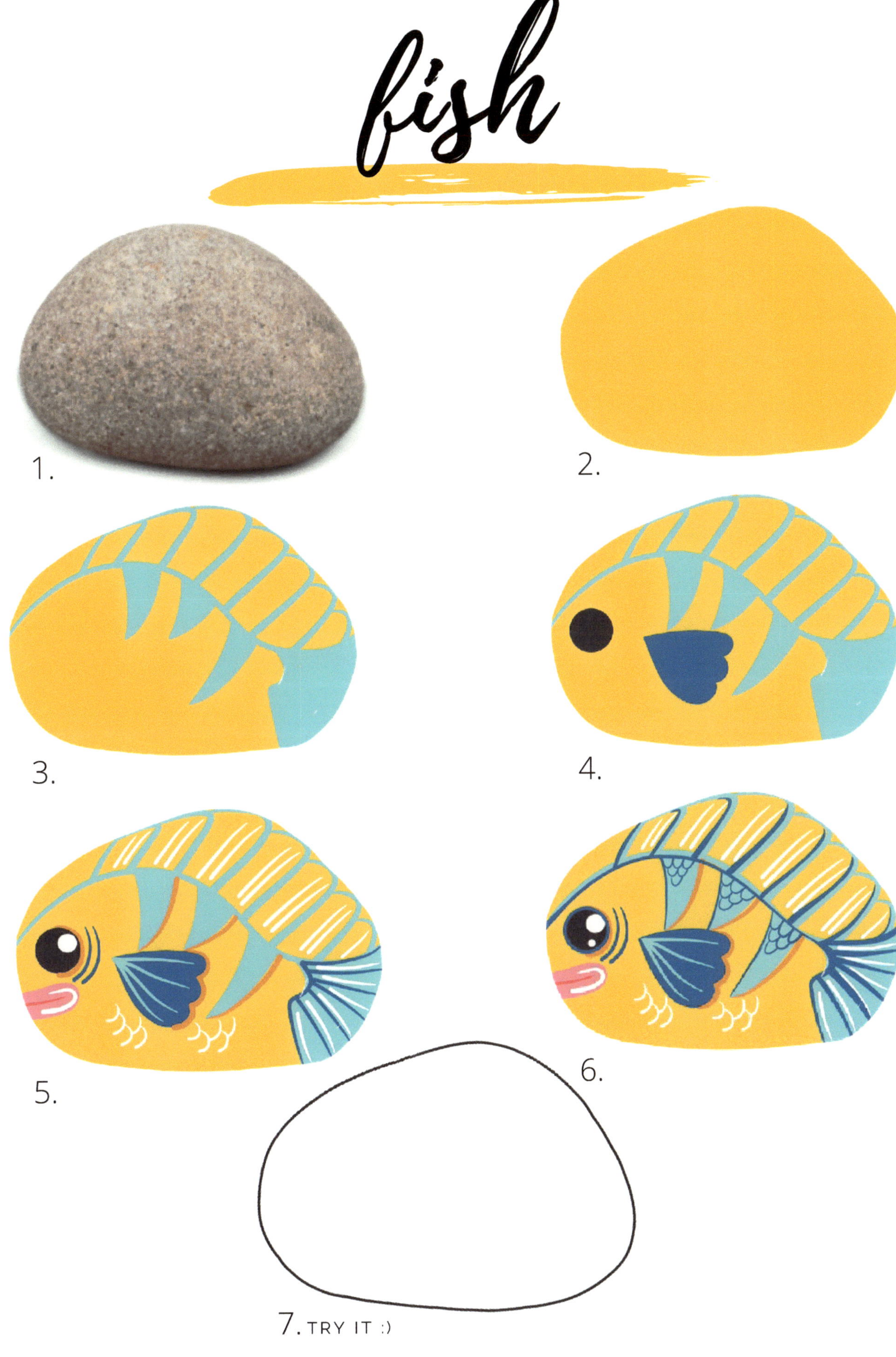

bird

feather

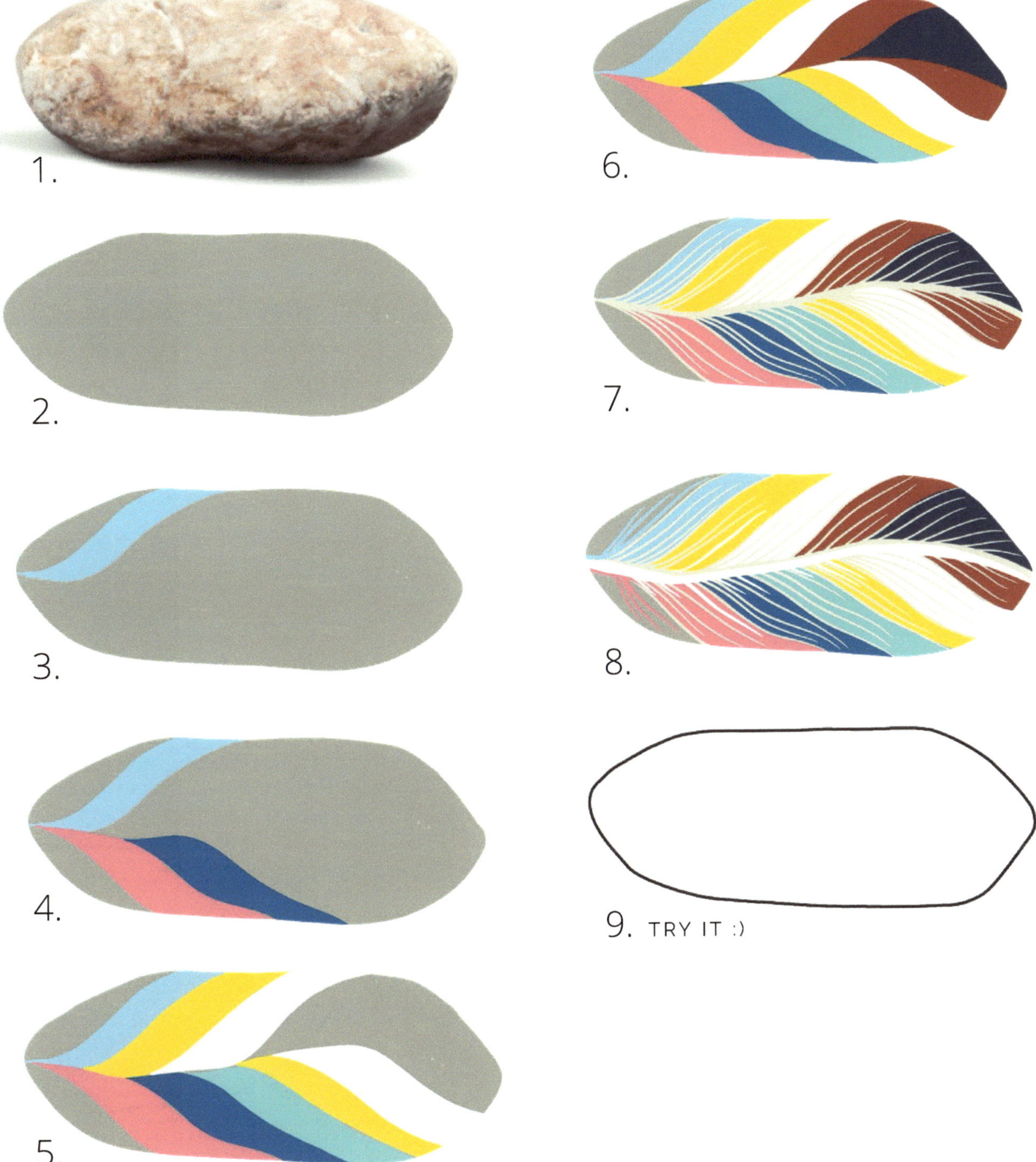

eye

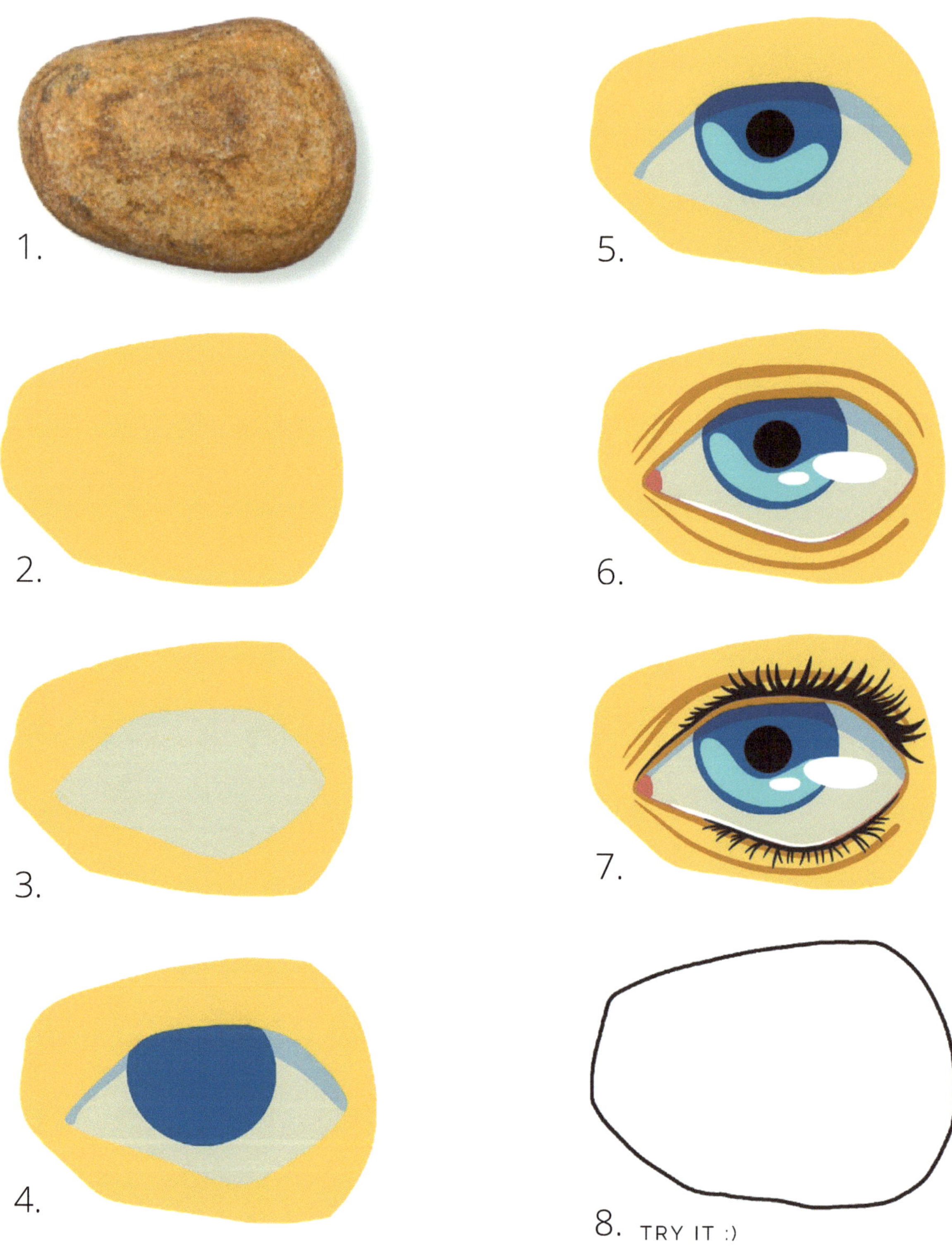

Eye from the reptile

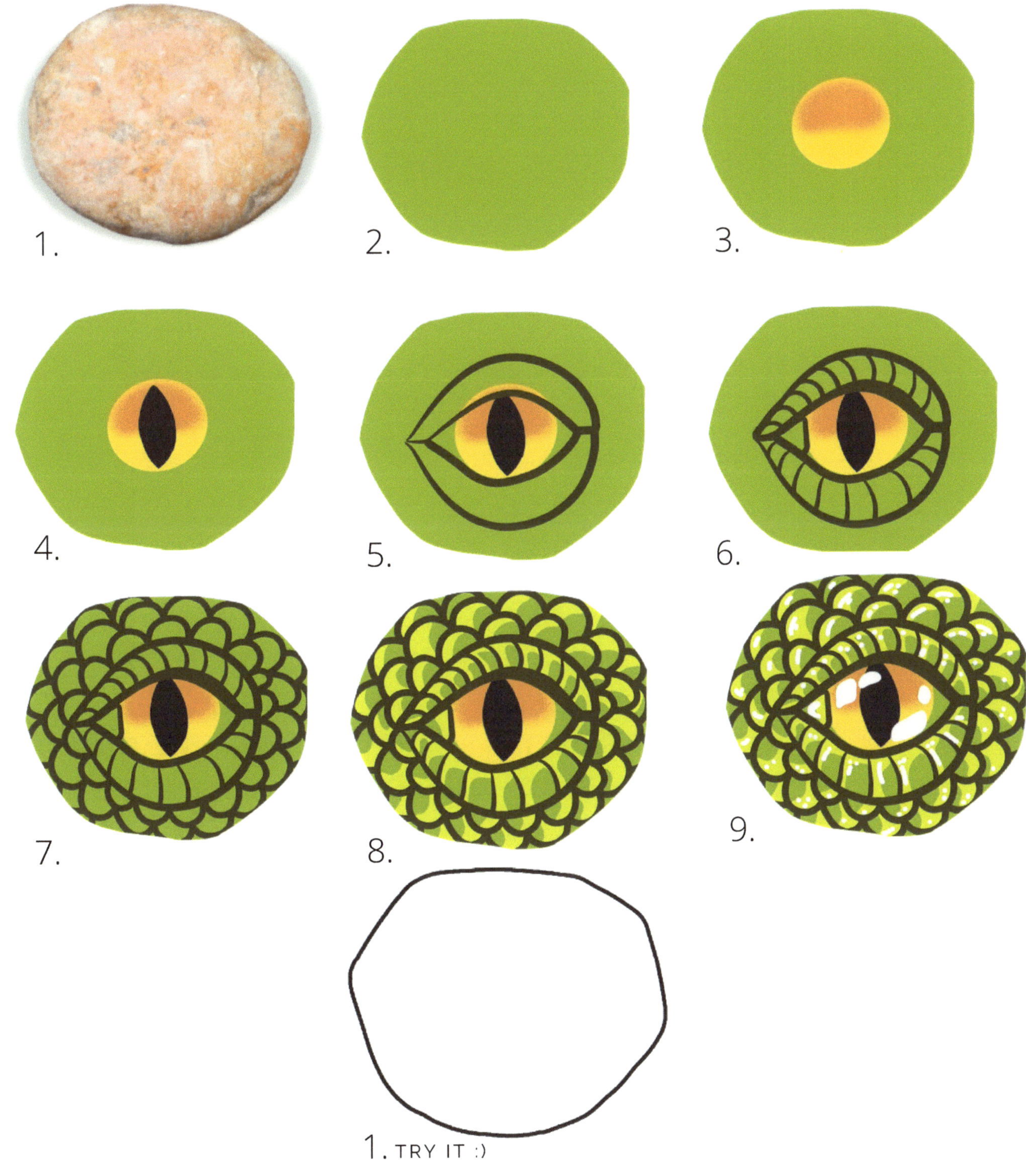

Dot Mandala

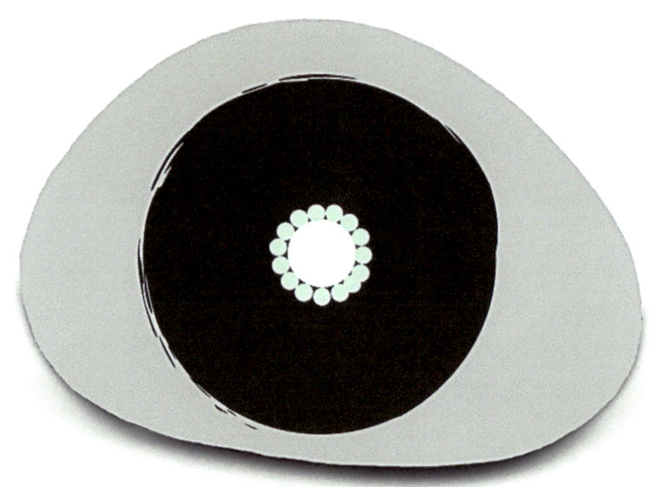

WE ALWAYS START WITH A LARGE POINT IN THE MIDDLE OF THE STONE, WHICH WE THEN SURROUND WITH SMALL POINTS.

IT IS ADVISABLE TO PAINT THE STONE BLACK SO THAT THE COLORS COME OUT BETTER.

A SPECIAL DOTTING TOOL IS BEST TO PAINT THE DOTS, BUT YOU CAN ALSO TEST THIN BRUSHES OR THE WHOLE THING FIRST WITH FELT-TIP PENS. COTTON SWABS ARE ALSO GOOD FOR THIS.

PAINT THE NEXT DOTS STAGGERED AND GET BIGGER AND BIGGER, START WITH THE LIGHTEST COLOR

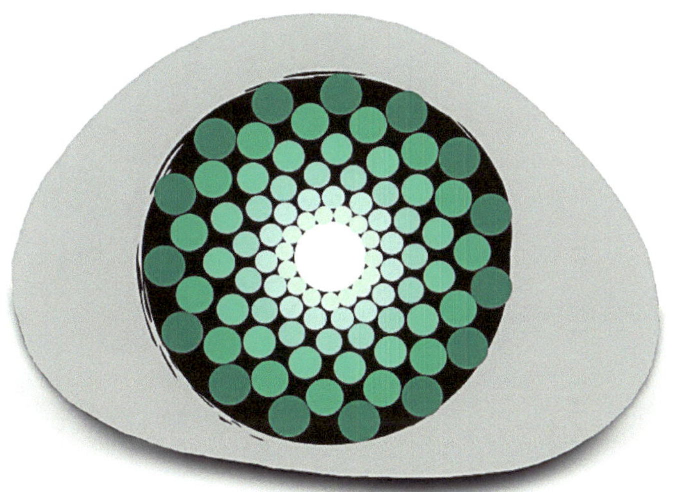

FILL THE WHOLE BLACK AREA WITH DOTS AND GET DARKER AND DARKER WITH THE COLOR

THE LAST POINTS HALFWAY OVER
THE BLACK BORDER.

SMALL DOTS IN THE SPACES.

POINTS IN POINTS WITH THE COLOR OF THE FRONT ROW.

A FEW MORE POINTS FOR DECORATION AND YOUR DOT MANDALA IS READY :)

PROBIER ES AUS :)

CONTACT: ANNEMEYER235@GMAIL.COM

www.ingramcontent.com/pod-product-compliance
Ingram Content Group UK Ltd.
Pitfield, Milton Keynes, MK11 3LW, UK
UKHW060121300726
14090UKWH00002B/305

* 9 7 9 8 7 2 4 1 5 9 8 8 3 *